Written by:
Coralyn Jones

leap!®

Illustrated by:
Reshonda D. Perryman

leap!

ORDERING INFORMATION

Leap! is available for bulk purchases for educational use. For details, send request to loveliveleap@gmail.com or contact Andrea Jones-Davis at 769-300-1122.

ISBN 10:0-9979731-3-7
ISBN 13: 978-0-99-79731-3-6

Dedication

For my mother, Andrea.

This book is dedicated to the fierce and fearless woman who continues to guide me through life. She has helped me grow into a great young woman who is unafraid of independence and has taught me to live my best life. Keep God First and Everything Else Will Fall In Place!

Here's to you, Mom!

Love,
Coralyn

Beautiful One, you are a dancer! You feel it in the beat of your heart. You're sure of it in your brain. From the top of your head to the tips of your toes, you are a dancer. So dance, my dear. Do it with character. Here are some things you'll need. When you possess them, you will leap to your destiny.

With fluid motion like water
you flow across the stage.
As you soar through the air
and move with ease, grace
is your name.

Grace

What do you want?

Who will you be?

Dream

You get to decide, so don't forget to dream.

Belie

Dream big, and believe it'll come true. There are lots of great things inside you.

Though you may be small now, there's always room to grow. Listen to many types of music.

Grow

Learn new styles of dance. Someday you'll see expanding your horizons will lead to great chance.

It's deep inside. You know it. You can be it. Who you're meant to be is more than just a feeling. You have purpose. It shows, and the world needs your flow.

Purpose

When your feet hit the stage and the rhythm touches your soul, you'll feel peace and release control of your worries and cares.

Peace

Faith

Have faith, Tiny Dancer, in all you can be. Keep sight of your goals, and soon you'll see that even the smallest faith can lead to the biggest leaps.

Don't give up. You were built
for this. Difficult times were
made for persistence.

Persiste

In you there's a strength
that you could never guess.
When times get tough,
Little One, just press.

If you're in it to win it, don't back down. Don't quit.

Commitm

Dance takes commitment. One day you'll be the talk of the town.

Live, Laugh & Leap

There are many tough things you must do to be the best you. Just remember to take care of you. Live well, love hard, and laugh long. All these things you'll need to finish strong.

leap!

About the Author
Coralyn Jones

Coralyn Jones is an award-winning dancer who has spent the majority of her youth pursuing her passion, dance. She is no stranger to the stage and is skilled in many genres; ballet, modern, contemporary, jazz, tap, and hip-hop; to name a few. Coralyn began her journey in higher education by studying dance at the University of Southern Mississippi, where she was a member of the Repertory Dance Company and the Dixie Darlings. Coralyn will continue pursuing her life's dream of studying dance at the University of the Arts, but more than anything she seeks to be an inspiration to children who desire to dance.

Leap! is for children of all ages and stages who, like Coralyn, dream of a life as a professional dancer. Here she shares the characteristics it takes to achieve those dreams and make their marks on the world.

www.ingramcontent.com/pod-product-compliance
Lightning Source LLC
Chambersburg PA
CBHW041429090426
42741CB00003B/100